FUN WITH
PAPER
PLANES

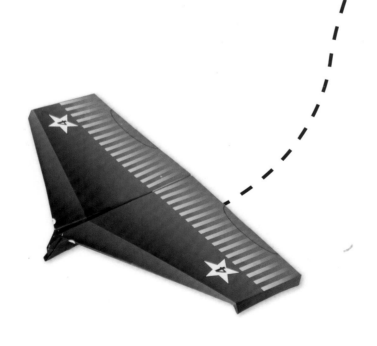

This edition published in 2019
By SpiceBox™
12171 Horseshoe Way,
Richmond, BC,
Canada V7A 4V4

First published in 2009
Copyright © SpiceBox™ 2009
Text copyright © ORCH Print Ltd P.

ISBN 13: 978-1-926567-33-4

CEO and Publisher: Ben Lotfi
Editorial: AnnMarie MacKinnon
Creative Director: Garett Chan
Art Director: Christine Covert
Design & Layout: Leslie Irvine, Owen Covert
Production: James Badger, Mell D'Clute
Sourcing: Tony Su, Carman Fung
Photography: James Badger
"**World Flyer**" World Record design created by Chris
Edge and British Aerospace Defence Ltd. engineers.
"**Delta Belter**" World Record design created by Andy
Currey and Guy Lomas (technical advisers, Chris
Vincent and Bob Ette).

ADULTS TAKE CARE
All the paper airplane designs featured are intended
to give great enjoyment and satisfaction, but the kit
contains a Power Launcher and elastic bands, which
can be used with paper clips, so please take care to
ensure that the airplanes are never aimed at any person
or animal and that children under eight years old are
supervised. The kit contains small components that could
be swallowed.

For more SpiceBox products and information, visit our
website: **www.spiceboxbooks.com**

Manufactured in China

9 10

CONTENTS

INTRODUCTION

All the designs in this book have been tried and tested over and over again, and I have placed them in their order of folding difficulty. This should help to make your enjoyment of folding paper aircraft progressive and fun. I have especially included instructions for the two World Record holders' for paper aircraft time aloft indoors, which both stayed up for an incredible 20.9 seconds. By the time you have worked your way through all 16 designs, you should be pretty good at building a wide range of paper aircraft that will amaze all your friends.

All you have to do is fold the sheets supplied according to the instructions beginning on page 6. There are four copies of each design in the kit. When you run out of sheets, because of loss or damage, you can easily make extra copies of the aircraft from the instructions, and color them in yourself if you wish. Also included are paper clips for use as weights, a Power Launcher and elastic bands, and decorative decals.

Now just get folding and flying, and you too could be a future World Record holder!

MATERIALS & TOOLS

You need very few tools to make the aircraft from the materials in the kit. Basically, all you need to do is fold them and fly them. But if you want to make extra models of these designs, or make your own designs, then the materials and tools listed here will be useful.

HOW TO USE THE DECALS

There is a pack of self-adhesive colored decals and "stickers" with a mix of different designs included in the kit. Just peel them off and place them in position as described here.

1. Try not to put too many on one aircraft, or they will weigh it down too much.

2. If you put one on one side, put another one the same size on the other side and in about the same position. Keep things balanced if you can.

3. On some of the designs there are positions marked to show where to place the decals. These are only guides. Place them where you feel they look good, without changing the way the aircraft flies.

4. If you run out of the printed decals just draw your own, like those in the kit, or make up your own design. Remember, if you press too hard with a pen, especially a ballpoint pen, you will crease the paper and change the way the aircraft flies.

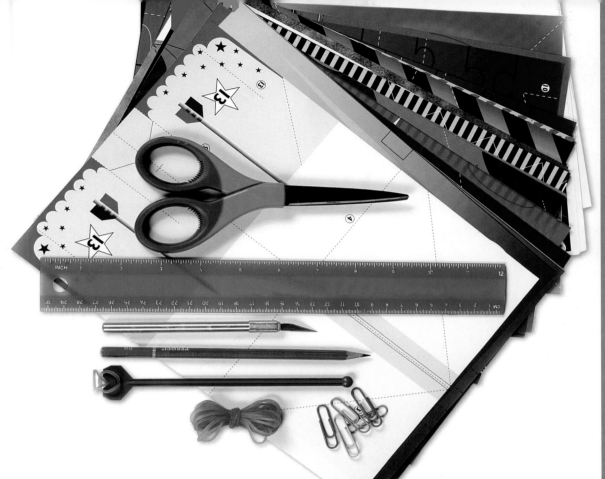

TOOLS

Rule
Scissors
Craft knife
Cutting mat
Pencil
Pen
Color felt tip pens
Sticky tape
Paper clips for weight and to make a Power Launcher
Power Launcher (supplied)
Right angle for checking the folds are straight
Rubber bands for the Power Launcher
Eraser

Note: Always get help from an adult when using a craft knife or sharp scissors.

MATERIALS & TOOLS

TYPES OF PAPER

Paper comes in many shapes, sizes and weights, but what works best for paper aircraft is a good quality paper that is clean, flat, dry and makes a good, crisp snapping sound when flicked on the edge.

You will find that all the aircraft in this book are slightly under the A4 or A5. That is simply to fit them into the kit; they are all on the same scale or ratio as A4. If you draw a line from the top right hand to the bottom left of a sheet of A4 paper and you mark a couple of points along the length of the line, you will find they are all the same ratio as one another: this is how the (A) standard of paper sizes works. However, don't worry if your paper is 8 ½ x 11 inch (216 x 280 mm); the designs will still fly. You may need to change the trim or you can make all the aircraft around the A5 size. You will be able to cut that size from A4 or 8 ½ x 11 inch paper. The correct paper weight depends on what type and what size of aircraft you are going to make. Paper aircraft make from paper sizes A5 to A4 or 8 ½ x 11 inch (216 x 280 mm) are best made from around 70 to 100 gsm weight paper. Very small paper aircraft made from paper sizes A8 to A6 are best made from lighter paper; 55 to 75 gsm works well.

PARTS OF A PLANE.

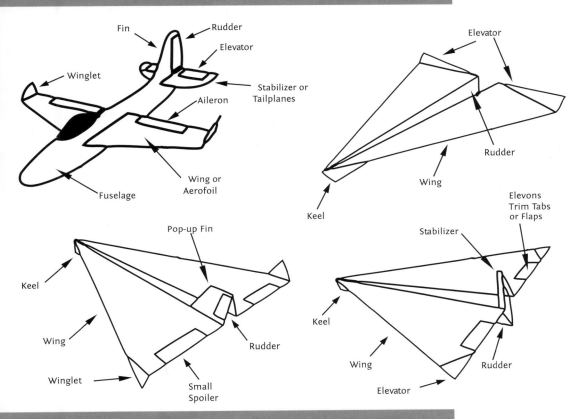

Fin
Rudder
Elevator
Winglet
Stabilizer or Tailplanes
Aileron
Fuselage
Wing or Aerofoil

Elevator
Rudder
Wing
Keel

Pop-up Fin
Keel
Wing
Winglet
Small Spoiler
Rudder

Elevons Trim Tabs or Flaps
Stabilizer
Keel
Wing
Elevator
Rudder

FOLD SYMBOLS.

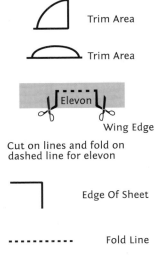

Trim Area

Trim Area

Elevon
Wing Edge

Cut on lines and fold on dashed line for elevon

Edge Of Sheet

Fold Line

1 2 3   Fold Line Numbers

Fold Line In That Direction

Unforld Line In That Direction

Fold And Unfold

T Turn Sheet Over

F Flip Sheet Over

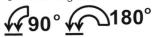 Drawing Numbers

Rotate Sheet counter clockwise 90 or 180 Degrees.

90°   180°

Push In or Up

Cut On Line

Tape Here

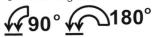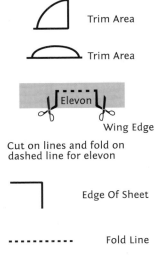

MATERIALS & TOOLS

1 SOLARWING

SIMPLE FOLD-OVER DESIGN WITH A SUPER LONG TAIL.

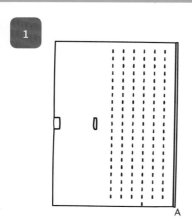

Cut off long tail (A) and put to one side.

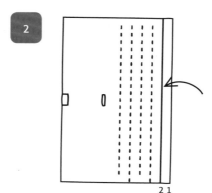

Fold on line 1 to line 2. Note: Be very careful to make good straight folds on all the following lines.

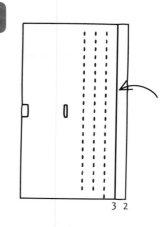

Fold on line 2 to line 3.

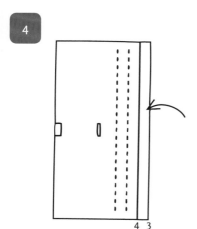

Fold on line 3 to line 4.

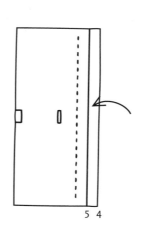

Fold on line 4 to line 5.

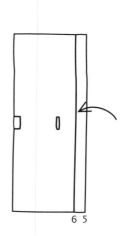

Fold on line 5 to line 6.

7

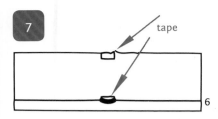

tape

6

Fold on line 6 and tape down at the position marked on the center of the wing. This will ensure the folds stay in place. You now have the leading edge.

8

Leading edge view:

Hold and pinch the center of the wing. Using your thumb and two fingers crease the leading edge. Bend up both ends of the wing a small amount to shape as shown. To check if it has been bent correctly, lay the wing "sun side up" and simply press down on the leading edge on one side. The other one should rise up by about 1 inch (25 mm). Don't be too fussy about this; it's just a guide.

9

Fit the tail on the center mark shown using a small piece of tape.

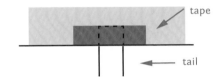

tape

tail

10

Put your SOLAR SUN FLYER decal where indicated so that the face is visible from the side, like this.

THROWING SOLARWING:

This simple fold-over design with a super long tail flies inside or outside. A standard throw is achieved by holding the Solarwing above your head, with a pinch grip between your thumb and index finger. Hold the leading edge where indicated, gently flick and release, but throw it forward and not downward (see drawing). It is best to use a gentle release action at first, and once you have mastered this, try throwing at a slight angle across your body. The Solarwing should band around and back toward you. This is a fun aircraft when launched from up high, but be careful. Keep away from any steep edges, and always have an adult to guide you.

THROWING SPEED: slow to medium.

2 INTRUDER

1

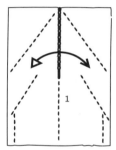

Fold on line 1.

2

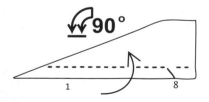

Fold on lines 2 and 3.
Note: Remember to leave a gap.

3

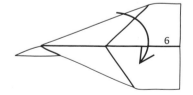

Fold on lines 4 and 5.
Note: Remember to leave a gap.

4

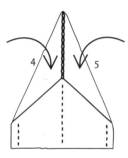

Rotate the sheet counterclockwise 90 degrees and refold up on line 1.
Note: Check that both sides are about the same size. Cut on line 8.

5

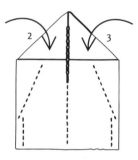

Fold down on line 6.
Note: Remember to leave a gap.

6

Turn the sheet over and fold down on line 7.

7

Fold up the winglets on lines 9 and 10, the same amount on each side. Open the keel section and push up the pop-up fin. Crease to form a diamond shape when viewed from the rear.

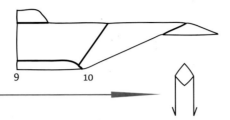

8

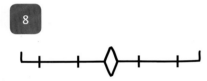

Cut Micro Trim Flaps, then open the wings out to an angle of 90 degrees. Now adjust the wing and winglet angles so that when viewed from the rear the aircraft looks like this. Move the Micro Trim Flaps up or down for fine trim control.

9

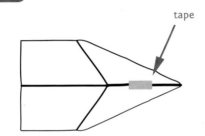

tape

Next close the keel together and apply tape on the area marked to hold the keel in position.

THROWING INTRUDER:

Throw as you would a dart at a dartboard, horizontally and straight out in front of you.

THROWING SPEED: slow to medium.

3 SUPERSONIC SKYRIDER

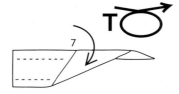

ADVANCED PASSENGER PLANE. POWER LAUNCHER ADAPTABLE.

1

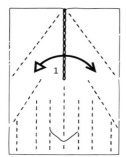

Fold on line 1 and unfold.

2

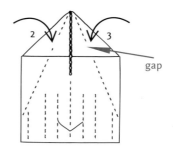

Fold on lines 2 and 3.
Note: Remember to leave a gap.

3

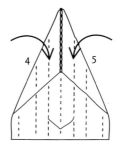

Fold on lines 4 and 5.
Note: Remember to leave a gap.

4

Rotate the sheet counter-clockwise 90 degrees and refold up on line 1. Next cut on line 12.
Note: Check that both sides are about the same size.

5

Fold down on line 6.

6

Turn the sheet over and fold down on line 7.

7

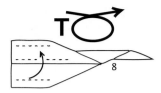

Fold up on line 8.

8

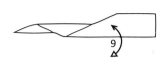

Turn over and fold up on line 9 then unfold both wings as in drawing detail.

9

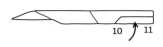

Fold the winglets on lines 10 and 11, then lift them up to an angle of 90 degrees to the main wing as in the drawing detail.

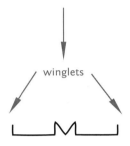

winglets

10

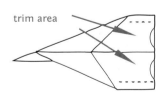

trim area

Push up the pop-up fin and re-crease on the central fold only. This is how it should look from the tail end. Note: Do not crease the two lower folds on the pop-up fin, as this helps keep the correct shape at the rear of the keel which tapers to the front.

SUPERSONIC SKYRIDER

TRIMMING

Trim the aircraft by "creasing up" with your finger and thumb, in the areas marked (trim area) at the rear of the wings.

THROWING SUPERSONIC SKYRIDER:

Throw as you would a dart at a dartboard, horizontally and straight out in front of you.

THROWING SPEED: medium to fast.

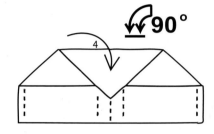

4 SUPERSNOOPER

BIG WINGED SPY PLANE WITH SPY CAMERAS.

1

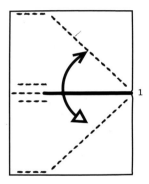

Fold on line 1 and unfold.

2

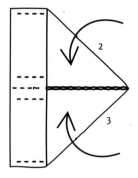

Fold on lines 2 and 3.
Note: Remember to leave a gap.

3

Rotate the sheet 90 degrees counterclockwise and fold down on line 4.

4

Fold down on lines 5 and 6. Note: Use a rule on lines 5 and 6 as the paper is quite thick.

5

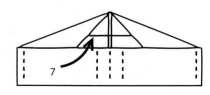

Fold up on line 7.

6

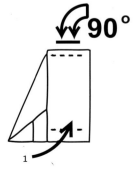

Turn the sheet over and rotate counterclockwise 90 degrees and fold up on the back of line 1.

7

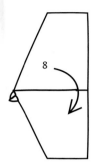

Fold down on line 8.

8

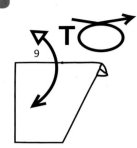

Turn the sheet over. Fold down on line 9 and then unfold.

9

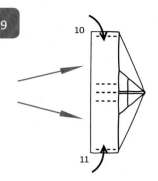

Fold the winglet lines 10 and 11 to an angle of 90 degrees.

10

Rear view just before throwing with the keel held together.

11

Rear view on work surface.

TRIMMING

Trim the aircraft by "creasing up" with your finger and thumb in the areas marked (trim area) at the rear of the wings.

THROWING SUPERSNOOPER:

Throw as you would a dart at a dartboard, horizontally and straight out in front of you.

THROWING SPEED: slow to medium.

CANARD TROOP TRANSPORTER

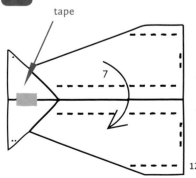

WITH FOUR WINGLETS.

1

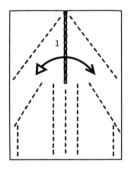

Fold on line 1 and unfold.

2

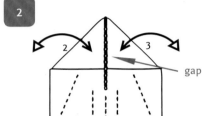

Fold on lines 2 and 3 and unfold again, then fold back on lines 2 and 3 so they are both behind the sheet.

3

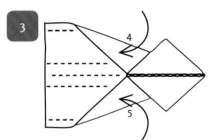

Fold on lines 4 and 5, being careful not to crease the triangle shapes made by folds 2 and 3. They should be allowed to flip out with ease and end up on top. It should now look like this.
Note: Remember to leave a gap.

4

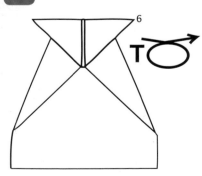

Turn the sheet over and fold on line 6.

5

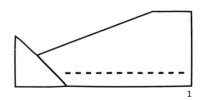

Turn the sheet over, rotate it counterclockwise 90 degrees and fold up on the back of line 1.

6

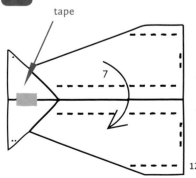

Fold down on line 7.
Note: Use a rule on this fold.

7

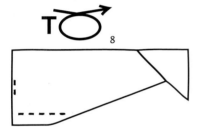

Turn sheet over and fold down on line 8.
Note: Start to fold line 8 at the nose end first as it's thicker.

8

Lift up both wings to an angle of 90 degrees to the keel. Turn the sheet over and fold in the front winglets 9 and 10 and the rear winglets 11 and 12 to an angle of 90 degrees to the main wing (see Fig. 6).

9

Next, hold the keel together and put tape where marked (see Fig. 6) to hold it in place.
Note: This tape position is where you should place the pilot decal.

THROWING CANARD TROOP TRANSPORTER:

Throw as you would a dart at a dartboard, horizontally and straight out in front of you.

THROWING SPEED: medium to fast.

THUNDERWING

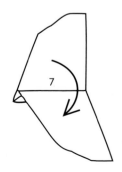

FIGHTER BOMBER, BIG WING WITH WINGLETS AND POP-UP FIN.

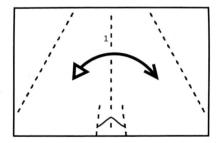

Fold on line 1 and unfold.

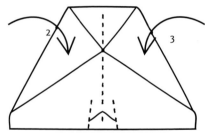

Fold on lines 2 and 3.

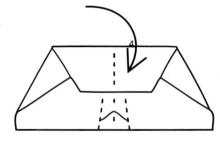

Fold down on line 4.

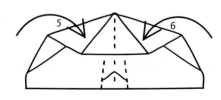

Fold down on lines 5 and 6.
Note: Use a rule to fold lines 5 and 6 as the paper is quite thick.

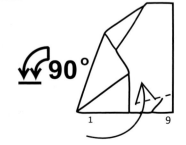

Turn the sheet over and rotate it counterclockwise 90 degrees. Fold up on the back of line 1 and cut on line 9.

Fold down on line 7.

7

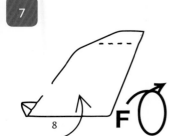

Flip the sheet over and fold up on line 8, ensuring that both sides are as equal as possible.

8

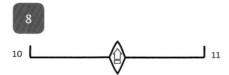

Unfold the wing to the shape above. Fold up on the winglet lines 10 and 11 to an angle of 90 degrees, and push up the pop-up fin.
Note: Do not forget to re-crease the fin area by pinching it on the folds and re-crease them to form a diamond shape when viewed from the rear.

9

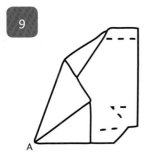

Lift the wings up and hold the nose at (A), and using your finger and thumb, re-crease the top of the keel in the pop-up fin area. Then fold the wings down again as in Fig. 10.

10

Rear view in flight:

Top view when laying on a flat surface:

Rear view just before throwing with keel held together:

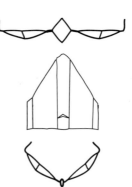

THROWING THUNDERWING:

Throw as you would a dart at a dartboard, but at a slight angle down from horizontal and with less force.

THROWING SPEED: slow to medium.

THE BAT

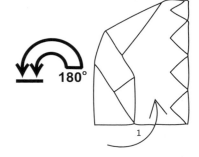

WW-SHAPED WING.

1

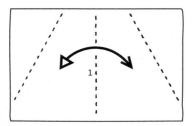

Fold on line 1 and unfold.

2

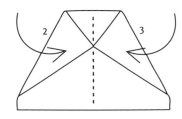

Fold on lines 2 and 3.

3

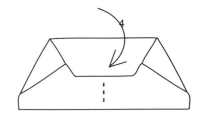

Fold down on line 4.

4

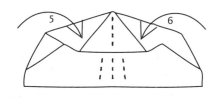

Fold down on lines 5 and 6.
Note: Use a rule on fold lines 5
and 6 as the paper is quite thick.

5

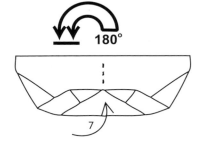

Rotate the sheet 180 degrees
and fold up on line 7.
Note: Use a rule on this fold.

6

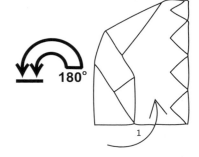

Rotate the sheet 180 degrees
and fold up on line 1.
Note: Use a rule on this fold.

7

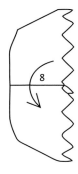

Fold down on line 8.
Note: Use a rule on fold line 8.

8

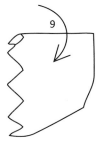

Turn the sheet over and fold down on line 9, ensuring that both sides are as even as possible.
Note: Use a rule on this fold.

9

Fold and unfold on lines 10 and 11 so that when laid on a flat surface it looks like this.

10

Front view: Just before launching with the keel held together.

11

Trim by lifting up or down on the rear saw lines.

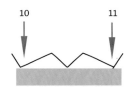

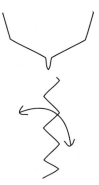

THE BAT

THROWING THE BAT:

Throw as you would a dart at a dartboard, horizontally and straight out in front of you.

THROWING SPEED: medium to fast.

DELTA BELTER

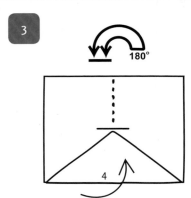

ANDY CURREY'S WORLD RECORD PLANE — POWER LAUNCHER ADAPTABLE.

1

Fold on line 1 and unfold.

2

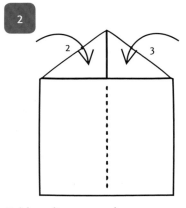

Fold on lines 2 and 3.
Note: there is no gap at the center line between folds 2 and 3.

3

Rotate the sheet counterclockwise 180 degrees and fold up on line 4 to mark on the center line.

4

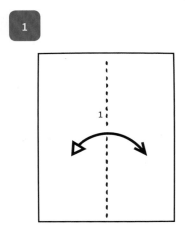

Fold in on lines 5 and 6.
Note: Make lighter creases on fold lines 5 and 6 to help give the wing some aerofoil shape.

5

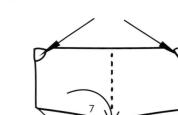

Fold down on the locking tab on line 7.

6

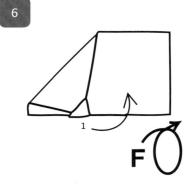

Flip the sheet over, rotate it counterclockwise 90 degrees and fold up on the back of line 1.

7

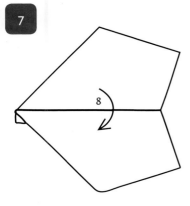

Fold down on line 8.

8

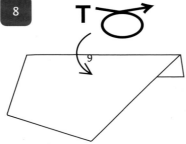

Turn the sheet over and fold down on line 9, ensuring that both sides are as even as possible.

9

This is how it should look from the tail end..

In hand:

Note: The profile is flat across both wings.

In flight:

Note: The pocket shape between the wing surfaces

10

Side view when held at the rear of the keel.

Note: The underside of the lower wing surface should hang down to the height of the locking tab like this:

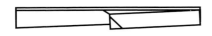

11

WORLD CHAMPION ANDY CURREY changes the keel height at the rear of the plane, from 1 inch (25 mm) for dry weather conditions to $1\,1/16$ inches (27 mm) for normal or wet conditions. The front keel also changes from $3/32$ inch (2 mm) in dry weather conditions to ¼ inch (6 mm) in normal or wet conditions. The standard heights are ¼ inch (6 mm) at the front and $1\,1/16$ inch (27 mm) at the rear.

This plane is designed to be made from A5 90-100 gsm paper, but it still works very well using standard lighter weight paper, such as 70 or 80 gsm.

TRIMMING

Trim the aircraft by "creasing up" with your finger and thumb in the areas marked (Trim Area) at the rear of the wings.

THROWING DELTA BELTER:

Throw as you would a dart at a dartboard, horizontally and straight out in front of you.

THROWING SPEED: slow to fast.

9 WHITE FLYER

CHRIS EDGE'S WORLD RECORD PLANE. POWER LAUNCHER ADAPTABLE.

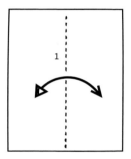

Fold on line 1 and unfold.

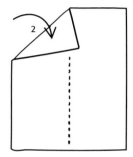

Fold on line 2.
Note: The fold overlaps the center line.

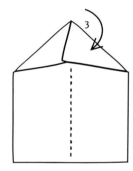

Fold on line 3.
Note: The fold overlaps fold 2 and the center line.

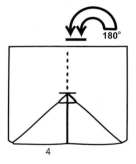

Rotate the sheet counter-clockwise 180 degrees and fold up on line 4 to mark on the center line.

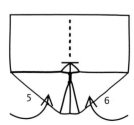

Fold on lines 5 and 6.

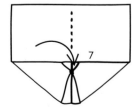

Fold down the locking tab on line 7.

7

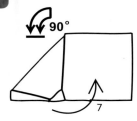

Flip the sheet over, rotate it counterclockwise 90 degrees and fold up on the back of line 1.

8

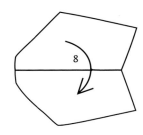

Fold down on line 8.

9

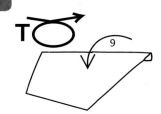

Turn the sheet over and fold down on line 9, ensuring that both sides are as even as possible.

10

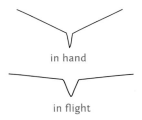

in hand

in flight

Note the large dihedral on this plane when the keel is held together, and very small dihedral when in flight.

11

trim area

Tape down on the four areas where indicated.

TRIMMING

Trim the aircraft by "creasing up" with your finger and thumb in the areas marked (Trim Area) at the rear of the wings.

THROWING WHITE FLYER:

Throw as you would a dart at a dartboard, horizontally and straight out in front of you.

THROWING SPEED: slow to fast.

10 STINGRAY

WITH SUPER LONG TAIL.

1

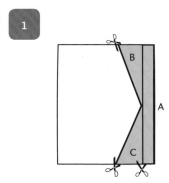

Cut off the long tail (A) and put it to one side, then cut off (B) and (C) and throw them away.

2

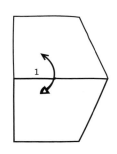

Fold on line 1 and unfold.

3

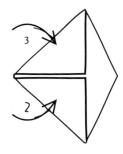

Fold on lines 2 and 3.
Note: Remember to leave a gap.

4

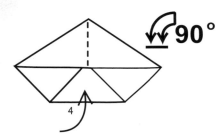

Rotate the sheet counterclockwise 90 degrees and fold up on line 4.

5

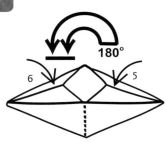

Rotate the sheet counterclockwise 180 degrees and fold down on lines 5 and 6.
Note: Use a rule on fold lines 5 and 6 as the paper is quite thick.

6

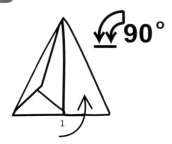

Turn the sheet over, rotate it counterclockwise 90 degrees and fold up on the back of line 1.

7

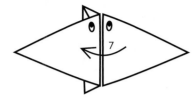

Rotate the sheet 90 degrees clockwise. Fold down on line 7.
Note: Use a rule on this fold as the paper is very thick at the front end.

8

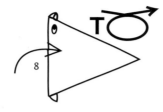

Turn the sheet over and fold down on line 8.
Note: Use a rule on this fold as the paper is quite thick.

9

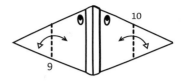

Lay the plane flat on the table and fold and unfold on lines 9 and 10.
Note: Use the guide marks on the keel to help with accuracy.

10

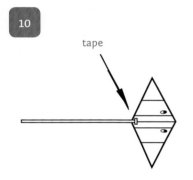

Open the plane up to expose the inside area of the keel and tape along one side only where indicated on the keel section.

11

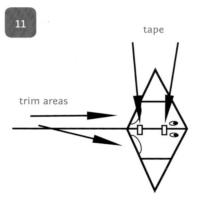

Next, hold the keel together and put tape where marked to hold it in place.

12

Note: The wing tips have an up angle that is easy to see, and the main wing area has a very slight anhedral.

STINGRAY

TRIMMING

Trim the aircraft by "creasing up" with your finger and thumb in the areas marked (Trim Area) at the rear of the wings.

THROWING STINGRAY:

Throw as you would a dart at a dartboard, horizontally and straight out in front of you.

THROWING SPEED: medium to fast.

11 SLOW FLOATER

WITH LARGE POP-UP STABILIZER.

This flies well indoors — especially in large sports centers or exhibition halls. It should be launched from high up in light or no wind conditions to achieve its best performance. This plane is a very good thermal indicator when flown outdoors.

1

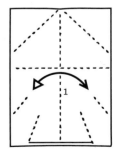

Fold on line 1 and unfold.

2

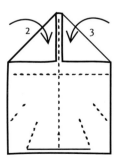

Fold on lines 2 and 3.
Note: Remember to leave a gap.

3

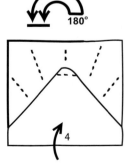

Rotate the sheet counterclockwise 180 degrees and fold up on line 4 to the mark on the center line.

4

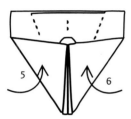

Fold in on lines 5 and 6.

5

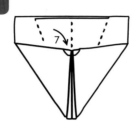

Fold down the locking tab on line 7. Flip the sheet over, rotate it counterclockwise 90 degrees and fold up on the back of line 1.

6

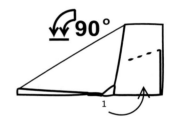

Fold down the locking tab on line 7.

7

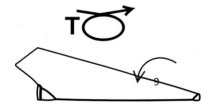

Flip the sheet over, rotate it counterclockwise 90 degrees and fold up on the back of line 1.

8

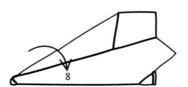

Turn the sheet over and fold down on line 9, ensuring that both sides are as even as possible.

CONTINUED.

9

Lift up both wings to allow room to cut on line 10 to make the pop-up Stabilizer. Open the keel, push up the Stabilizer and re-crease to form a diamond shape as in the drawing below.

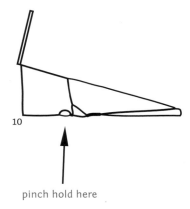

pinch hold here

10

Note: The correct way to hold this for throwing is to pinch with the thumb and tip of the index finger, just behind the locking tab on the keel. Point the nose of the plane slightly down and use a slow dart-type throw. Keep the keel open at all times, then gently release.

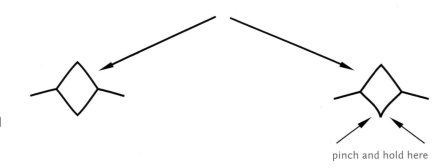

pinch and hold here

11

Top view in flight, showing the pop-up Stabilizer in the correct position.

Note: When using the pinch hold to throw, the top view should look the same as in flight. To adjust the trim, move the elevators on the rear of the main wing up or down to correct the flight path.

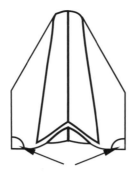

trim area

12

Extra trim control can be obtained by adjusting the wing angle up or down.

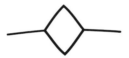

TRIMMING

Trim the aircraft by "creasing up" with your finger and thumb in the areas marked (Trim Area) at the rear of the wings.

THROWING SLOW FLOATER:

Throw as a slow dart type, and keep a pinch hold just behind the locking tab of the keel. Point the nose of the plane slightly down from the horizontal, keeping the keel open at all times, then gently release.

THROWING SPEED: medium to fast.

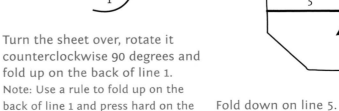

12 CRAZY STUNT SPECIAL

WITH ELEVONS AND WINGLETS, POWER LAUNCHER ADAPTABLE.

1

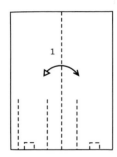

Fold on line 1 and unfold.

2

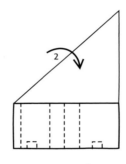

Fold on line 2.

3

Fold on line 3.

4

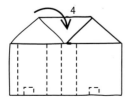

Fold down on line 4.

5

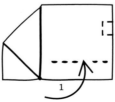

Turn the sheet over, rotate it counterclockwise 90 degrees and fold up on the back of line 1. Note: Use a rule to fold up on the back of line 1 and press hard on the nose as the paper is quite thick.

6

Fold down on line 5.
Note: Use a rule on this fold.

7

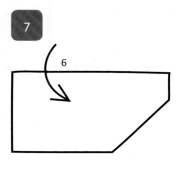

Turn the sheet over and fold down on line 6.
Note: Use a rule on this fold.

8

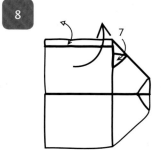

Unfold on line 6. Fold down on line 7. Fold and unfold the winglet on line 8.

9

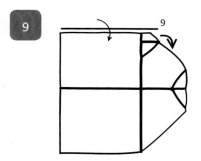

Unfold on line 7. Fold on line 9, unfold to an angle of 90 degrees and fold the winglet on line 8 again to an angle of 90 degrees

Front view on work surface.

Front view in hand.

10

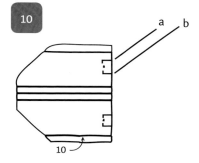

Top view on work surface.

Turn the sheet over and fold the winglet on line 10. Unfold the winglet on line 10 to an angle of 90 degrees. Cut on (A) and (B) lines on both wings for crazy stunt elevons and fold up.
Note: This winglet folds in the opposite direction to the other winglet.

THROWING CRAZY STUNT SPECIAL:

Throw in almost any direction you like as its flight path tends to be, by design, quite erratic. Try an angle of 85 degrees from horizontal for your first throw.

THROWING SPEED: medium to fast.

13 INTERCEPTOR

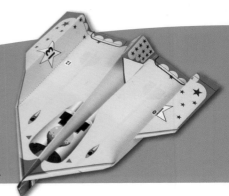

SUPERFAST DEFENDER, POWER LAUNCHER ADAPTABLE.

1

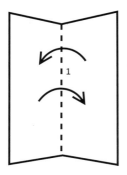

Fold on line 1 and unfold.

2

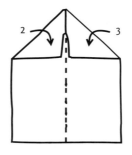

Fold on lines 2 and 3.
Note: Remember to leave a gap.

3

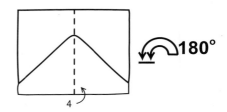

Rotate the sheet counterclockwise 180 degrees and fold up on line 4 to the mark on the center line.

4

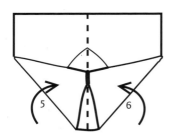

Fold in on lines 5 and 6.

5

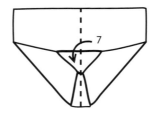

Fold down the locking tab on line 7.

6

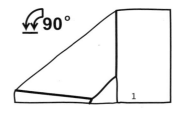

Flip the sheet over, rotate it counterclockwise 90 degrees and fold up on the back of line 1.

7

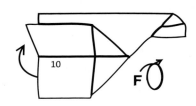

Fold down on line 8

8

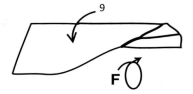

Flip the sheet over and fold down on line 9.

9

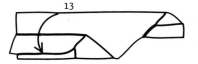

Flip the sheet over and fold up on line 10.

10

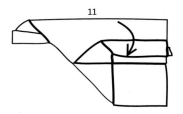

Fold down the same wing on line 11.

11

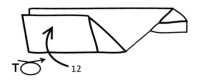

Turn the sheet over and fold up on line 12.

12

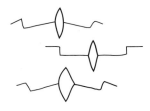

Fold down the same wing on line 13.

13

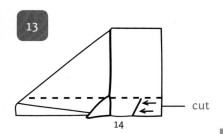

Lift up both wings to allow room to cut on line 14 to make the pop-up fin. Open the keel section, push up the pop-up fin and re-crease to form a diamond shape when viewed from the rear.

14

Now trim the wing angles so that from the rear of the aircraft it looks like this:

THROWING INTERCEPTOR:

Throw as you would a dart at a dartboard, horizontally and straight out in front of you.

THROWING SPEED: medium to fast.

14 JIGSAW

JIGSAW CAMOUFLAGE PATTERN ALL OVER, AND LARGE FINS.

1

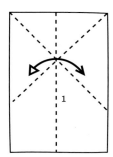

Fold on line 1 and unfold.

2

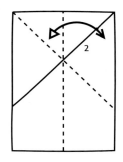

Fold on line 2 and unfold.

3

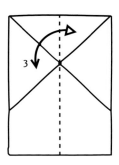

Fold on line 3 and unfold.

4

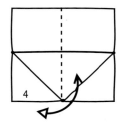

Turn the sheet over, rotate it counterclockwise 180 degrees. Fold up on line 4 and unfold.

5

Lift up.

Carry on lifting until both edges touch. Next push forward both edges.

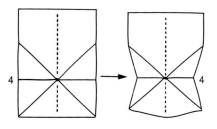

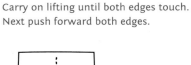

Turn the sheet over. Lift up on both the edges of fold 4.

Done. It should now look like this.

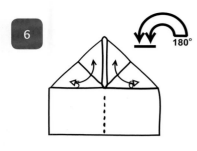

6

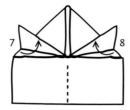

7

Rotate the sheet counter-clockwise 180 degrees. Fold up on lines 5 and 6 and unfold.
Note: Remember to leave a gap.

Fold up on lines 7 and 8.

8

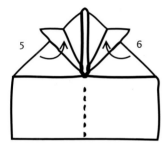

9

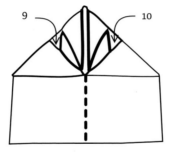

Fold up on lines 5 and 6 again.

Fold down on lines 9 and 10.

10

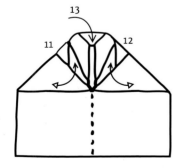

11

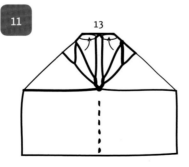

Fold in on lines 11 and 12 and unfold. Fold down on line 13.

Lift up fold 13 to an angle of 45 degrees and push open the two pockets in the edges of the fold, using your index fingers.

JIGSAW

CONTINUED.

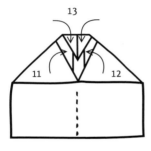

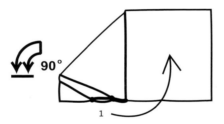

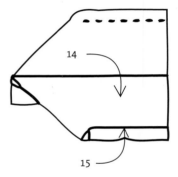

Fold in again on lines 11 and 12, tucking the edges into the pockets made by the fold on line 13.
Note: You will have trapped folds 9 and 10 underneath folds 11 and 12. This is correct. Press down hard on these folds to lock them down in place.

Turn the sheet over, rotate it 90 degrees counterclockwise and fold up on the back of line 1.

Fold down on line 14 and up on line 15.

15

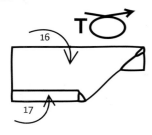

Turn the sheet over and fold down on line 16 and up on line 17.

Top view on flat surface:

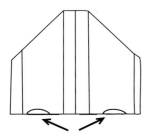

16

With the keel held together lift up both wings to form a "V" shape. Next lift up both winglets to an angle of 90 degrees to the main wing. Your Jigsaw should now look like this:

Rear view just before throwing with keel held together:

Move the wing angle up or down for extra trim.

TRIMMING

Trim the aircraft by "creasing up" with your finger and thumb in the areas marked (Trim Area) at the rear of the wings.

THROWING JIGSAW:

Throw as you would a dart at a dartboard, horizontally and straight out in front of you.

THROWING SPEED: slow to fast.

JIGSAW

SPACE AGE FLYER, POWER LAUNCHER ADAPTABLE.

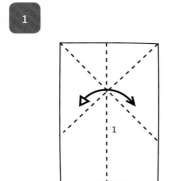

Fold on line 1 and unfold.

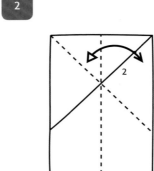

Fold on line 2 and unfold.

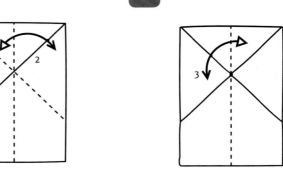

Fold on line 3 and unfold.

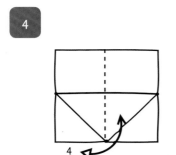

Turn the sheet over, rotate it counterclockwise 180 degrees. Fold up on line 4 and unfold.

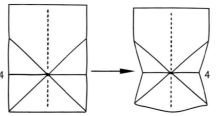

Lift up.

Carry on lifting until both edges touch. Next push forward both edges.

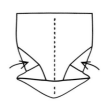
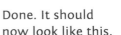

Turn the sheet over. Lift up on both the edges of fold 4.

Done. It should now look like this.

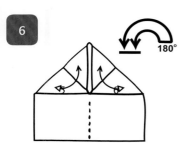

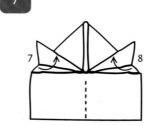

Rotate the sheet counter-clockwise 180 degrees. Fold up on lines 5 and 6 and unfold.
Note: Remember to leave a gap.

Fold up on lines 8 and 9.

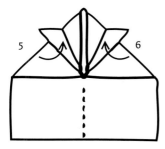

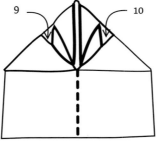

Fold up on lines 5 and 6 again.

Fold down on lines 9 and 10.

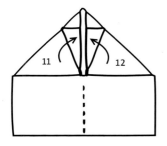

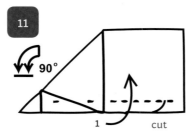

Fold in on lines 11 and 12, trapping the folds made by lines 9 and 10.

Turn the sheet over, rotate it counterclockwise 90 degrees and fold up on the back of line 1. Next, cut the curved shape on line 13 and push up the pop-up fin. Re-crease to form a diamond shape when viewed from the rear.

CONTINUED.

12

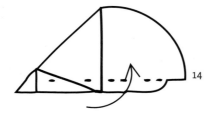

13

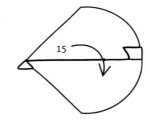

14

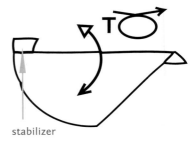

Holding the keel and wings together, cut off the curved shape on line 14.
Note: Be careful to ensure the wings do not move when cutting.

Fold down on line 15 and pop up the stabilizer.

Turn the sheet over, use a rule again to fold down on line 16 and unfold both wings as in diagram 15.

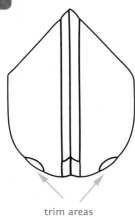

trim areas

Your Nazca Flyer should now look like this.

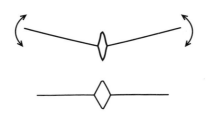

Extra trim control can be obtained by adjusting the wing angle up or down.

The wings should be almost level during flight.

NAZCA FLYER

TRIMMING

The Nazca Flyer requires fine-tuning to fly correctly, but once trimmed it flies like a dream. Trim the aircraft by "creasing up" with your finger and thumb in the areas marked (Trim Area) at the rear of the wings.

THROWING NAZCA FLYER:

Throw as you would a dart at a dartboard, horizontally and straight out in front of you.

THROWING SPEED: slow to fast.

16 SONIC IMPULSE

TWIN SONIC POWERED HI-TECH LIFTER, WITH POP-UP FIN, POWER LAUNCHER ADAPTABLE.

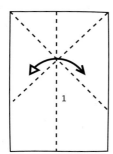

Fold on line 1 and unfold.

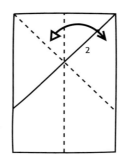

Fold on line 2 and unfold.

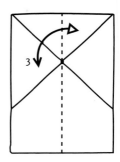

Fold on line 3 and unfold.

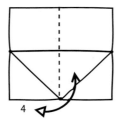

Turn the sheet over, rotate it counterclockwise 180 degrees. Fold up on line 4 and unfold.

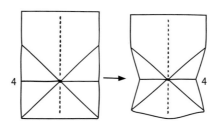

Turn the sheet over. Lift up on both the edges of fold 4.

Lift up.

Carry on lifting until both edges touch. Next push forward both edges.

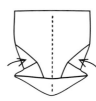

Done. It should now look like this.

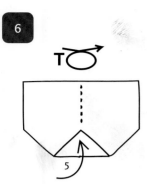

6

Turn the sheet over and fold up on line 5.

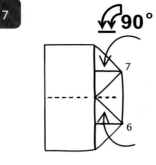

7

90°

Turn the sheet over, rotate it counterclockwise 90 degrees. Fold on lines 6 and 7.

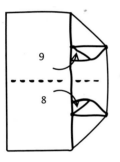

8

Fold on lines 8 and 9.

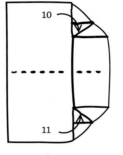

9

Unfold folds 9, 8, 7, and 6. Fold on lines 10 and 11.

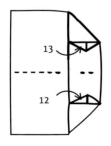

10

Unfold folds 11 and 10. Fold on lines 6 and 7 again. Fold on lines 12 and 13.

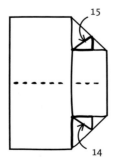

11

Unfold folds 13, 12, 6, and 7. Fold on lines 14 and 15.

CONTINUED.

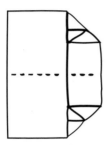

12

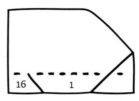

13

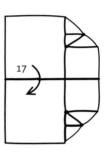

14

Unfold 14 and 15.

Fold up on line 1 again. Cut on line 16.

Fold down on line 17.
Note: Use a rule on this fold as the paper is quite thick in the nose area.

Turn the sheet over and fold down on line 18.
Note: Use a rule on this fold.

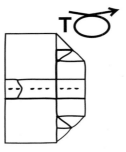

Unfold line 18 and turn the sheet over. Open the keel section and lay the plane flat on your work surface.

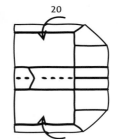

Lift up folds 6 and 7 to an angle of 90 degrees. Fold on winglet lines 19 and 20.

18

Re-form the keel by running your index finger and thumb along the keel bottom. Push up the pop-up fin and re-crease to form a diamond shape. Lift up the winglets 19 and 20 to an angle of 90 degrees to the main wing. Adjust the main wings so they are at 90 degrees to the keel section. When the keel is held together at the nose, your Sonic Impulse should look like this from the rear view:

19

Top view on your work surface:

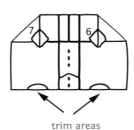

trim areas

rear view

front view in flight

TRIMMING

Trim the aircraft by "creasing up" with your finger and thumb in the areas marked (Trim Area) at the rear of the wings.

THROWING SONIC IMPULSE:

Throw as you would a dart at a dartboard, horizontally and straight out in front of you.

THROWING SPEED: slow to fast.

It takes time to trim this one but once correct it will fly upside down very well. It is also good at tail slides and will do great vertical launches, where it can fall over backwards and loop back into normal flight.

THROWING TECHNIQUES

Most paper aircraft need only a gentle throw when flying indoors, at a slight angle down from horizontal to start them off. With others, the throw required is so light that it feels like you are almost just letting them go.

Paper aircraft are normally designed with a degree of built-in stability and, provided they are trimmed correctly, will glide gracefully away after launching. Most people tend to throw all paper aircraft at the same speed, usually too hard and too fast, causing the aircraft to both distort out of shape and become un-aerodynamic. This normally produces a stall and the aircraft crashes. The person throwing them usually blames the aircraft.

There are some paper aircraft that are designed to stall: the Crazy Stunt Special is one such design. This aerobatic aircraft will flip over, tail slide, stall and roll without any problems.

If attempting a "time-aloft" record in a large indoor area, then the aircraft will need to be thrown with great force straight up, but it will also need to be specially designed for this flight plan.

LOOK OUT — LOW FLYING AIRCRAFT!

If you are flying indoors and there is anything in the room that could break, like a china tea set, then be warned: all paper aircraft will seek them out and hit them. If there is a heavy cupboard that you can't move, paper aircraft will find a way to hide behind it and be just out of reach so you can't get them back.

Make it a rule always to use a checklist:

1. Think of what you are trying to achieve before you pick up the aircraft.

2. Assess what the weather conditions are like, and if the aircraft is capable of flying in these conditions.

3. Check that the aircraft is ready for flight; look the aircraft over for damage; set the trim and wing angles, etc.

4. Think safety. Have a good look around to make sure that it's all clear before you throw. This is a very important check, and is always the last thing you should do before any flight. If you follow this checklist every time, you will be a better pilot.

THROWN-INDUCED STRESS DISORDER.

No one wants to get "thrown-induced stress disorder" in an aircraft, and throwing it harder than it's designed to be thrown, or throwing it incorrectly, are good ways to get it.

So what is "thrown-induced stress disorder"? Imagine for a moment the paper aircraft is three feet (1 m) long, all of it scaled up in size, except the paper thickness, which remains the same. This will make it easier to visualize the effects of poor handling. One movement too quick, when you pick it up, or throwing too hard, and it will fold up. Let us suppose that it has been thrown too hard, and now has a large crease in the keel area. This is going

THROWING TECHNIQUES

to be an obvious weak point, which will fail during any kind of flight. This demonstrates that it is not what can be seen that is the problem, it's what can't be seen. Small creases, lines or buckles can be caused by over-stressing, but can also be caused in other ways: for example, folding incorrectly, or impact damage due to a crash landing.

FLYING INDOORS.

Indoors, the air tends to be quite still. In these predictable conditions you have a greater opportunity to test-fly and trim the aircraft properly and get it flying well. It is best not to have windows or outside doors open to avoid creating varying air currents.

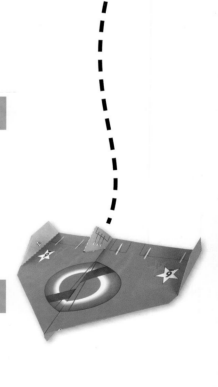

FLYING OUTDOORS.

Flying outdoors with paper aircraft is very unpredictable. With such a light aircraft the wind has a big effect on how it flies, and you never know what the wind will come up with next. Sometimes it will catch the aircraft and send it up out of sight; other times it will smash it to the ground. It's not worth fighting the wind with a paper aircraft: you're better off using the wind to help you.

The weather is constantly changing, and on good days you can find that thermal winds will help the aircraft fly. These are rising bubbles of warm air caused by the sun heating up the ground and, indirectly, the air above the ground.

TEN COMMON PROBLEMS WITH PAPER AIRCRAFT.

1. Folds are not symmetrical (i.e., not the same on each side).

2. You did not check the shape of the aircraft before it was thrown.

3. Aircraft thrown too hard or too soft.

4. Aircraft thrown at the wrong angle, too high or too low.

5. Aircraft thrown in an arc from the elbow. You should throw as if your hand is attached to a curtain rail, straight from the elbow.

6. Wind is too strong for the type of aircraft you are trying to fly.

7. Trim area is not set correctly; set too much or set the wrong way.

8. Wing angle is too high or too low; check design drawings.

9. Wings are bent by bad folding or by crash landing, from a damp atmosphere, by being picked up by wing instead of the keel, or because paper not stored flat before folding.

10. Paper is too thick or too thin for design of aircraft and flying conditions.

THROWING TECHNIQUES

First, find a large grass field or open park area. Find out which way the wind is blowing and how strong. To do this, hold some grass up in the air, let it go and see which way it floats. If it drops to the ground close to you, then you have light wind conditions. However, if it flies off at 90 degrees, then the wind is too strong.

What you are after is a wind that will carry the grass away at about an angle of 40 to 50 degrees. If the angle is more than 50 degrees, use paper clips on the nose or use the Power Launcher as shown on the following pages.

Unless the wind is very light, it is always best to throw across the wind rather than into it or downwind. Using this technique, the aircraft will normally turn downward, roll and stay banked over, as it flies off and picks up speed downwind. Being banked over at an angle, an aircraft with speed will produce a natural turn, back into the wind.

By this time, the aircraft will have traveled quite some way downwind, and should have gained some height in doing so. If the wind speed and the air speed of the aircraft match as it turns back into the wind, the aircraft will hover like a bird on the wind. Eventually the wind speed will change just enough to alter the angle and the speed at which the aircraft is flying, bringing it in to land.

PAPERCLIPS: USE AND EFFECT.

You can help the aircraft attack the wind by adding weight to its nose. Use metal paper clips for this. They are easy to put on and take off again. Place one or two paper clips in the nose area, on one or both sides of the lower part of the keel, ensuring that the keel remains open if the design requires it. If the wind is blowing one minute and not the next, you can take the paper clips on and off to suit the conditions.

Always throw harder when the wind is blowing. Expect to re-trim or re-shape the wings on the aircraft after adding any extra weight. Test flights are an important part of learning how to become a good paper aircraft pilot.

PAPER FATIGUE.

Fatigue, or getting tired, is not only a problem for us humans, it happens to paper aircraft as well.
The most common causes are:

1. Throwing the aircraft too many times.

2. Crashing the aircraft too many times, especially if re-shaping is required.

3. Keeping the aircraft in a damp environment. Don't fly your aircraft in the rain, on damp cold evenings, or in foggy weather.

4. Continually picking the aircraft up by anything other than the keel.

5. Transporting the aircraft to the flying site in a soft bag where it could become bent and will need to be re-creased on the main wing folds. This can make the main wing folds very weak and the whole aircraft become prone to flapping instead of flying. If you spot this problem, ditch the aircraft and build a new one.

6. Throwing the aircraft too hard or at the wrong angle, so that it bends out of shape. It then dives out of control, using up all the wing fold strength. When recovering, these folds become fatigued and end up limp and floppy instead of crisp and trim.

THROWING TECHNIQUES

THE POWER LAUNCHER

WHERE TO USE IT.

The best way to beat the wind is to join it up high and with speed. With the Power Launcher you can do this.

The Power Launcher is for use outside in a large field or open park and not indoors, since the aircraft will fly so fast that the flight would be over in seconds. The Power Launcher works best if you use the elastic bands as shown in the diagram on page 57.

POWER LAUNCHER AND AIRCRAFT TRIM.

Never trim a Power Launcher aircraft so that it flies correctly indoors. This is because the extra weight of the paper clip, when flown at slow speed, will give too much lift when flying at high speed; wait until you get outside to trim the aircraft. After the first test flight outside you will discover how the aircraft flies, and then you will be able to set the trim.

To make the paper clip connector and adapt the aircraft you need a medium-size paper clip, 1 ¼ inches (30 mm). If you haven't got this exact size that's okay, but don't try to use the super large ones that are 2 inches (50 mm) long, since they tend to be too heavy.

Start with the paper clip as shown. The letters are marked counterclockwise on this drawing to make it clear where each of the hold and bend positions are.

Hold the paper clip at E and D. Bend H down past the line made by C and D at a 45 degree angle.

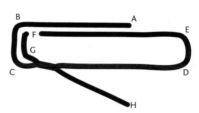

Hold the paper clip at B and C. Pull down on H until F touches the line made by C and D.

Note: You may have to pull down F past the line made by C and D to overcome any spring effect you may find. This is quite normal. You have now made the hook.

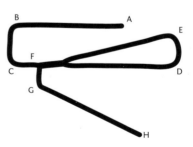

When using the Power Launcher, launch the aircraft across the wind rather than downwind. If you do fly into the wind, launch the aircraft with the nose at a lower angle, about 20 to 30 degrees. This will allow the aircraft to fly at maximum speed and to overcome the wind speed for long enough to gain some height, turn and then glide down.

THE POWER LAUNCHER

ATTACHING THE POWER LAUNCHER HOOK.

1

Hold the aircraft in your right hand the correct way up. Open the keel of the aircraft and point the nose toward the hook.

2

Hold the hook at B and C and place only E, D and F inside the open keel section. At this point, A and H should be hidden behind the keel and B and C should be sticking out in front of the aircraft nose. B and C are used for crash protection.

3

Tape the hook in position, covering up and across F, E and D only.

4

Close the keel section back together and re-shape the wings into the correct normal flying position.

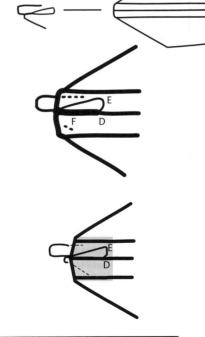

Note: The elastic band should be hooked over H and rest on G, ready for the launch. Hold the aircraft keel at the position shown and, after stretching the rubber bands, aim up as per the instructions on page 56 and gently release.

MAKING A PAPER HOOK.

There is another way to make a hook, in the paper aircraft itself, which works very well. This paper hook is normally used in light winds as it weighs less than the "paper clip hook." If you want to use the paper hook in strong winds, you can use a small metal washer as ballast. Tape it inside the keel at the nose. Or you can use a small twig if you have nothing else suitable.

1

Mark a point on the keel center line 1 $\frac{1}{2}$ inches (40 mm) from the nose of the aircraft. Place a piece of 1 inch
(25 mm) wide sticky tape across the keel, with the tape center on the 1 $\frac{1}{2}$ inches (40 mm) mark, so that it starts and finishes just below the wings on each side.

2

Make two cuts, as shown, to form a notch in the lower part of the taped keel, at a slight angle towards the nose. The notch should be a maximum of $\frac{5}{16}$ inch (8 mm) deep and $\frac{3}{16}$ inch (5 mm) wide at the opening, going to a point at the top. The top helps reinforce the keel section that has just been cut.

Use the Power Launcher in the same way as the paper clip hook.

THE POWER LAUNCHER

HOW TO USE THE POWER LAUNCHER.

First, never point the aircraft at any person or animal. Hold the Power Launcher in one hand with your arm stretched out and up at an angle between 20 and 60 degrees, with the aircraft attached to the rubber bands at the other end. Pull the aircraft all the way back to your hip before releasing it. When launching, use a long, slow pull and gently release the aircraft on the Power Launcher.

When you have got used to using your Power Launcher, try using it at an angle of between 60 and 90 degrees. This prevents the wings from distorting outside of the aircraft's flight envelope ("flight envelope" defines the limits within which the aircraft can physically fly before becoming out of control).

You will need to experiment with the number of bands you use on the Power Launcher because the power of the launch is dependent on the type of bands you have, their thickness and length, etc. The trick is to have enough bands to allow the Launcher to gently launch the aircraft and not bend it out of shape as soon as it is released. Remember, you will require a lot of space to use a paper aircraft adapted for Power Launch.

SUPERTIPS

Over time you will find that there is a lot more to making paper aircraft than meets the eye, especially if you are in competitions. Just a few adjustments can make all the difference when it comes to performance flying. Here are some Supertips, that will allow you to get the best results out of your paper aircraft.

1. FOLDING SURFACES.

One of the best surfaces for making paper aircraft is a cutting mat. Never fold on a soft, rough or uneven surface since this gives uneven creases that ruin the symmetry (evenness) of the aircraft. The best cutting mats are usually green with a grid pattern on them. They are available at good art shops.

2. SYMMETRY.

Make the folds on your aircraft as symmetrical as possible (the same on both sides). This will decrease the amount of trim required and, as a result, lessen any trim-induced drag and delay the inevitable landing.

3.CREASE FLATTENING.

Use your thumbnail as a tool for flattening out a crease when making a fold. Be careful not to overdo it since it's easy to press too hard and crumple or bow the paper, destroying the rigid flat surface and overall strength of the wing.

4. FOLDING.

When creasing on fold lines, especially thick ones, try using a rule to help to keep the folds straight. Take the rule and place it against the paper in the area you wish to fold. Pull the paper up against the rule edge and press your fingers along the edge of the paper. Run your fingers up and down the length of the fold, pressing down hard. This establishes the main part of the fold, and ensures that it is started off in the correct place. Next, remove the rule and press down firmly, running your fingers once again along the length of the partly folded sheet. Neatly finish off the fold, being very careful that you keep to the fold line.

SUPERTIPS

SUPERTIPS

5. THE GAP.

Try not to fold two edges over so that they touch at the center line: generally, leave a gap. If they do touch, when you come to make more folds the edges will press against each other, distorting the aircraft out of line. This means you will have to make more trimming adjustments later. The more trimming an aircraft has, the slower it will fly because of increased drag of the trim tabs or flaps. Look at how some of the designs in this book use "the gap".

6. POP-UP FIN.

Cut a line in the main keel from the bottom to the top. Push the cut section up from the bottom and crease it into position. This will make a great fin which will give rigidity and help control flight stability.

7. THE STABILIZER.

Cut a narrow strip $1/8$ inch (2-3 mm wide) at the rear of the main keel section, from the bottom to the top of the keel. Carefully push the cut section up from the bottom and crease into position. This will provide some speed control, light rudder adjustment, keel movement, shock absorption and anti-dive control too. It works well with wide-bodied aircraft, which normally fly slowly, but it also helps mid-speed aircraft as well.

8. MID-WING POP-UPS.

These are made in the same way as "pop-up fins", but they act more like a wing support or stiffener, rather than changing the way the plane flies. They are cut into a wing fold or winglet which would benefit from having some extra stiffening. Make them by cutting in two places, then creasing and folding a small section upward, usually in the center of the wing or on the creased edge of a wing which has an extra fold in it.

The Interceptor is a good example, because it has an extra fold in both wings where "mid-wing pop-ups" can be used.

If required, several "mid-wing pop-ups" may be cut along the wing, but don't have too many of them as they can slow the aircraft down.

Warning: They can also make the wing less stiff. If the "mid-wing pop-up" folds get fatigued, bend them into place only once.

SUPERTIPS

9. MICRO-KEEL TAB.

This simple fold is made by bending a small area $1/4$ inch
(6 mm) long at the lower rear corner of the keel, at an angle of 45
degrees left and then right. With the keel area creased, push up
toward the top of the keel section to form the micro-keel tab.

This works in two ways. First, it helps to keep the keel area open;
and second, it acts as a trim tab device, with upward pitch effect
due to its position on the keel section. The use of the micro-keel
tab will also slightly increase the width of the keel opening, so
some readjustment of the wing angle may be needed.

10. WHERE NOT TO FLY.

Don't fly in an alleyway, since the air rushes through and allows no
clean air for your aircraft to fly in. It gives the same effect as flying in
a wooded area; the trees cause a disturbance of the airflow. It is one
of the reasons that airports are usually built in large open areas.

11. THROWING OUTSIDE IN THE WIND.

As a general rule, if it is very windy then fly your aircraft indoors. If you do fly your aircraft outdoors, in a light wind, throw across the wind and never into it, unless you have a weight on the nose, such as a paperclip.

12. FLYING FROM UP HIGH.

Do all your initial testing indoors and if your aircraft flies well when you're standing on a chair, for instance, that's good, but don't be surprised if you have to change your trim settings slightly, when you fly from up high. This is normal. The reason for this is that when indoors the distance you can normally fly limits your flight speed, unless you are flying in a large indoor area.

Outdoors, the flying speed can be much greater. As the speed increases, the wing shape will change, which will alter the flight path. It will be necessary to do a few test flights from up high, just to get the wing angle and trim setting correct. Changing the wing angle can have a dramatic effect on how your aircraft flies. Once these settings are completed, your aircraft should look fantastic in flight, and all your hard work will have paid off.

Warning: Whenever you fly from a height, take extreme care especially if standing on a chair. Make sure you have permission from an adult.

13. PICKING UP YOUR AIRCRAFT.

After you have thrown your aircraft and it has landed, always pick it up by the thickest part of the keel section since this straight area is designed to support the wings. If you pick up your aircraft by a wing or winglet it may bend because it is not designed to carry the weight of the keel and the opposite wing. If you crease or fatigue that wing your aircraft could become damaged and unbalanced.

SUPERTIPS

14. MAKING A SMALL CHANGE.

It is very nice to have a long, straight flight, but it is often more likely that your aircraft will turn off to one side rather than fly straight. This is usually just a trim problem which, if left unchecked before any big flights, will turn from being a small out-of-trim into a big out-of-control. Time and again you will find that making just the smallest of bends on a wing, or a small pinch or two in a rudder area, will greatly improve flight performance, especially if you're flying from up high.

15. WHAT TO DO AFTER A CRASH.

If your aircraft has just crashed straight into the ground at high speed, or had a heavy impact on one wing you can expect to have to re-trim or re-shape it. Check the wing shape for symmetry (evenness on both sides); if the damage is too severe you will have to ditch the aircraft and start again. If it lands in very wet grass, a puddle or a stream, ditch it straight away: paper absorbs water very well and loses its shape and stiffness in doing so.

16. STUNT FLYING.

Stunt aircraft use the elevons as their main control surfaces. With these simple cuts in the rear of the delta wing area, you can fine-trim your stunt plane so that it performs some real stunts, like looping the loop, barrel rolls, tail slides and, best of all, finally banking at some amazing angle and then crash landing. Stunt paper aircraft are designed to be tough enough to crash-land, so a lot of fun can be had without worrying about what happens to them.

17. DESIGNING NEW AIRCRAFT.

If you do design your own aircraft, keep them simple, so that you can reproduce many test models for flight testing and minor modifications. If you become good at aircraft design you will be able to predict and therefore take advantage of any changes in wing angle that take place as the plane slows down. These changes may be achieved by slightly fatiguing the main keel fold (folding backward and forward on the same fold line to weaken it) so that the keel relaxes back to a normal flying shape in time for the flight task you are attempting. If you are designing a plane for time aloft or distance records, remember that the plane should be strong enough to survive a hard throw.

SETTING UP COMPETITIONS

Paper aircraft competitions are held all over the world and these competitions are open to people of all ages. That's the fun with paper aircraft: there is no real restriction. We all like making and flying them. You don't even have to join a formal club or organization. You can hold paper aircraft competitions with your friends.

WHERE TO FLY.

The first thing to do is to decide where you are going to hold the competition. All you need is somewhere that is large enough to fly. This could be your back garden or yard, in the hallway or your bedroom. One of the best places if the weather is good is the local park, schoolyard or playground. If you can use the gymnasium at school then that's a really good place.

THE JUDGE.

Decide who the judge is to be, perhaps someone who is not taking part. He or she should become well versed in the rules, which you and your friends can make up if you like, or follow the guidelines below. The judge has to be fair, and must be prepared for lots of excitement. And remember—you and your friend must abide by his or her decisions.

LAYING OUT A COMPETITION SHEET.

Draw out a record sheet on some paper, like the competition sheet shown on page 68. You can add extra categories from the list of ideas shown on the competition sheet.

PRIZES.

You can compete just for fun, but it could be more exciting if there are prizes to be won. Work out what the prizes are going to be. Bear in mind that you will need 13 prizes if you have 10 events as you will have 10 event winners and 1st, 2nd, and 3rd placed overall winners. To start off with, limit the number of events run to just four and only hand out prizes to the 1st, 2nd, and 3rd place overall winners. That way you only have three prizes to hand out. This gets you used to running competitions and you could have more events next time.

OFFICIAL CERTIFICATE.

You could even design your own certificate, giving it an official name, such as your own paper aircraft club.

THE LEAGUE.

If all your friends get hooked on paper aircraft, make up your own league, with monthly champions and end-year champions, and prizes purchased from funds raised by entrance fees.

CHARITIES.

Using paper aircraft competitions to raise money for a good cause is easy and worthwhile. Charge all competitors a fee for entering the competition and perhaps a smaller fee for each aircraft thrown. You could use pre-purchased raffle tickets, which each competitor hands in before they make their throw. Prizes could be given and the cash raised proudly handed over to the charity representatives, who should be invited along to help run the event. They could act as extra judges, or help sell the tickets to the competitors.

SETTING UP COMPETITIONS

DIFFERENT TYPES OF EVENTS.

Here is a list of the different types of events that you could have in a paper aircraft competition. You could use one or all of them for a large competition.

TIME ALOFT   The longest time in the air. Each competitor has 10 attempts; the best time of the day wins. Another way to run this event is to add together all 10 throws and the person with the most time aloft overall wins. This is a popular way to run this event because it prevents one lucky throw from winning the day and gives everyone a fair chance. Ideally, you would have a stopwatch for this event.

DISTANCE   The longest distance wins, and again, you could split this event into best of 10 throws added together. You should have a long tape measure, or you can pace out the distance by the number of large footsteps or shoe distances.

HIT THE TARGET   This is a knockout competition and whoever misses the target is out. You can make the target anything, like a football or a fence post (or the target inside the kit supplied with this book).

ALL IN A BOX   Everyone starts with at least 10 aircraft and writes his or her name or number on each one. The 10 aircraft are now placed in a pile in front of them. To start, everyone stands at a single point with the box at a distance of about 10 to 15 feet (3-5 m) away. Everyone then counts out aloud down from 10. On zero, everyone throws as fast as possible and all at the same time, until all the aircraft have been thrown. Competitors are allowed to throw only the aircraft that are in the pile in front of them, and no one moves until all the aircraft have been thrown. The person with the most of his or her aircraft in the box at the end is the winner. This event is a lot of fun: some aircraft will hit each other, while others will get knocked into the box by another competitor's aircraft.

BEST-LOOKING AIRCRAFT The best-looking aircraft that actually flies on the day wins this event. This is not necessarily the best-flying aircraft. Everyone can be the judge with this event and you could have another event for the worst-looking aircraft!

SPOT LANDING Draw or paint a large red spot on the center of a sheet of white card (or use the target inside the kit supplied with this book). The winner is whoever lands his or her aircraft on the red spot the most number of times. The aircraft has to land on or be touching the red spot, or skid over it. You could use different distances, depending on the ages of the competitors.

THROUGH THE HOOP Hang a hoop in a tree and see who can get their aircraft through it. You could set the number of attempts at this, or put up two hoops. A washing line works well for hanging hoops from if you don't have a tree. If you don't have a hoop, you can use a metal coat hanger bent in the middle to make a hoop shape.

AEROBATICS This is an event to decide the best stunt aircraft or stunt pilot. The winner is the competitor whose aircraft can loop the loop or do perfect tail slides, or is the best at overall aerobatics. This event will require a good judge to decide if the loop the loop was a good one or not. Remember, it is the judge's opinion that counts in this event, and not the competitor's. Don't argue with judges; you may need them later on!

HIGHEST FLIGHT The winner is the competitor whose aircraft flies the highest. You could have separate events with and without the Power Launcher. These events will require a good judge who can decide whose aircraft flies the highest if the difference is 6 feet (2 m) or less.

ALL THE SAME In this event, everyone builds the same design of aircraft and then you decide amongst yourselves what event you would all like to fly in; for instance, the longest distance or time aloft wins the event.

HOW TO

BECOME A WORLD RECORD HOLDER.

It is no accident that most of the record holders in the world of paper aircraft have some connection with the aircraft industry. Most of them, while in school, used to make and fly the classic dart-type of plane in some form or another. Some of the record holders are students in aerospace engineering. Do they have an unfair advantage? Well, not really, apart from their strong love and interest in all kinds of flight. They all know the general rules of aerodynamics, but none of them have been to college to learn about paper aircraft.

TIME-ALOFT CHAMPIONS.

Here we will look only at what it takes to be come a champion in the time-aloft duration class. We can split what is needed into four areas, with percentages for each. If you have what it takes, you may all meet up one day at a world record challenge event.

Champions like Ken Blackburn have inspired many hundreds of thousands of people all over the world with their achievements with paper aircraft. Ken would like to get his crown back, since he held the time-aloft duration record for many years. Ken is capable of beating the current record of 20.9 seconds, but Andy Currey, when he threw one of Chris Edge's fine-tuned paper aircraft, achieved an unofficial time of over 23 seconds.

Soon we could see 25 seconds. How long will it be before the 30-second barrier is smashed? And who will do it? Chris Edge, known as the Professor, Andy Currey, known as the Wild One, Ken Blackburn, known as Mr. Nice Guy? Or will it be you?

AREA 1 — DESIGN OF THE AIRCRAFT: 33%

Both of the current world champions' designs have been included in this book for you to build. They are very similar in their design, yet they are different in their construction. One common goal often produces very similar solutions. With both the designs to hand, you are now already 33% of the way there.

AREA 2 — HOW YOU BUILD IT: 33%

This shows how important precise folding and the way you build your aircraft are if you want to be a world champion. The former world champion for time-aloft, American Ken Blackburn, seems to fold from the heart; he knows his folds forward and backward and requires little more than a good sheet of paper. The same can be said for one of the current world champions, Briton Andy Currey, who will make 10 or more aircraft quite fast before he gets one he likes and then BANG, up it goes towards the rafters of the aircraft hangars. The other current world champion, another Briton, Chris Edge, will work with a computer-aided design and a dedication to repeatable tests. Small step-by-step improvements in the design, just on a simple fold, may change by a few thousandths of an inch and get his aircraft just right on the day. You won't find Chris Edge winning any speed-building prizes!

AREA 3 — HOW YOU THROW IT: 33%

All the world champions use the same type of throwing technique. Start off in a crouched position with your knees slightly bent and with your hand well back. Then, like a big, coiled spring, fling your hand up into the air. Use the whole of your body to power yourself up and at the last moment release, trying to keep the throw as straight up as possible, maybe just one degree off the vertical but not much more. If you get it right, then you're in with a chance of the world record. You now have 99% of the information needed to help you.

AREA 4 — THE UNKNOWN: 1%

This is the unknown part: not even the world champions know what it is. They just know they all have it. It could be that one degree angle on launch, or their accurate folding skills. With some of them it is working out carefully what seems to help, and with others it's just natural talent.

INDEX

INDEX

INDEX

INDEX

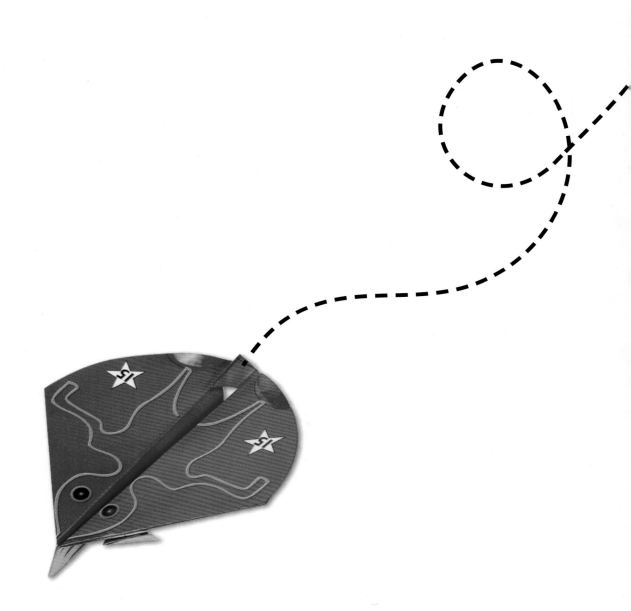